EXTRATERRESTRIAL
LIFE

Are Extraterrestrials a Threat to Humankind?

Toney Allman

ReferencePoint
Press®

San Diego, CA

© 2012 ReferencePoint Press, Inc.
Printed in the United States

For more information, contact:
ReferencePoint Press, Inc.
PO Box 27779
San Diego, CA 92198
www.ReferencePointPress.com

LIBRARY OF CONGRESS CATALOGING-IN-PUBLICATION DATA

Allman, Toney.
  Are extraterrestrials a threat to humankind? / by Toney Allman.
    p. cm. — (Extraterrestrial life series)
  Includes bibliographical references and index.
  ISBN-13: 978-1-60152-170-5 (hardback)
  ISBN-10: 1-60152-170-7 (hardback)
  1. Human-alien encounters. I. Title.
  BF2050.A38 2011
  001.942—dc22

                                                        2010046621

CONTENTS

Unknown Dangers

On an Earthlike planet circling its sun at just the right distance for an atmosphere to be possible and liquid water to flow, life develops. If humankind could reach that rocky world, they might discover creatures both eerily familiar and startlingly alien. That life might be single-celled and primitive or complex and brainy. It might even be sentient, conscious and self-aware, and intelligent, like human beings. Identifying such a planet, especially in a nearby star system, is within the capability of human science today. Traveling to the planet might be beyond current capabilities, but perhaps in the near future robots or probes could go and send data back to Earth. What would they find?

One possible scenario is imagined in the Discovery Channel's production *Alien Planet*. Based on the science-fiction book *Expedition* by Wayne Barlowe, the imaginary story of exploring an alien, life-filled world describes a virtual mission of exploration in a way that is as scientifically plausible as possible. A group of world-renowned scientists imagine that they are future scientists, analyzing and interpreting the information sent back to Earth by future state-of-the art robots and probes that are exploring the fictional planet Darwin IV.

A Virtual Mission to Another World

Darwin IV lies 6.5 light years from Earth, close by in terms of the size of the Milky Way galaxy that is home to both planets but far distant in terms of human space travel. The mother ship, named the *Von Braun*, which carried the exploratory robots and probes to Darwin IV, traveled for 42 years at 37,000 miles per second (59,545.728 km/s) or 20 percent of the speed of light (186,000 miles per second or 299,792.458 km/s) before it settled into orbit around the alien planet.

Since digital transmissions by laser beam—at the speed of light—from Darwin IV to Earth take 6.5 years, the mother ship, robots, and probes had to be built to be as independent as possible and to make decisions without human help. Ike and Leo, the two robots sent to the surface of the planet, are programmed to have the intelligence of human preschoolers—to see, hear, move, and manipulate objects, and to communicate their experiences to the mother ship. The mother ship carries an array of complex supercomputers that not only send all the data they collect to scientists on Earth but also reprogram the robots depending on the conditions on Darwin IV. Explains NASA chief scientist James Garvin, one member of the scientific group involved in the virtual mission, "Our first forays beyond the solar system will be robotic. They ought to be robotic. It makes sense. And we will be the bystanders much more so than we are today with our robotic emissaries. But that's okay . . . they'll act more like us in the sense that they'll observe, mine the data, understand the anomalies, the excitement, [and] find the sweet spots. And as they go, they'll open the door and our eyes to how we may go"[1]

> ### DID YOU KNOW?
>
> Today's fastest spacecraft can fly at only .00005 the speed of light, or about 36,000 miles per hour (57,936 kmph).

Abounding in Alien Life

Darwin IV's original mission scientists expected to find only microscopic life on the alien planet, since microscopic life is thought to be the

The starry Milky Way galaxy and scattered nebulae (dark areas) dominate the night sky above the three massive telescopes atop Hawaii's Mauna Kea volcano. Within the Milky Way galaxy lie mysteries that fuel both imagination and research.

most likely form of life in the galaxy, but they prepared for any eventuality. It was a fortunate decision because Ike and Leo soon discover a planet teeming with life. Darwin IV is smaller than Earth and has a thicker, denser atmosphere and lower gravity, and so its life-forms have evolved in startling ways. Many of its creatures, both small and large, use gas-filled bladders (somewhat like balloons) and biological jet propulsion for locomotion and to support their bodies. Flying animals suck the sap of "trees," and giant seven-story life-forms with mouths on their feet absorb nutrition from a gelatin "sea." And predators have evolved, too, just as they have on Earth. Physicist Michio Kaku explains, "Chances are, when we meet intelligent life forms in outer space, they're going to be descended from predators."[2] The predator animals of Darwin IV are evolved and smart: Some can cooperate and hunt in packs; others are ambush hunters the size of *Tyrannosaurus rex*.

Leo and Ike fly above the planet's ground to stay safe from the many dangerous animals and release small, expendable miniprobes to gather data. The two robots also extend

> ## DID YOU KNOW?
> Scientists estimate that the Milky Way galaxy is about 100,000 light years in diameter and consists of about 100 billion stars.

a greeting when they make the monumental discovery of true intelligent, sentient life. At the same time, they release miniprobes to assess any threat. The aliens probably think they are being attacked, however, and they destroy the robots. The signal stream to the mother ship ends abruptly. The mission scientists back on Earth—who were babies when the *Von Braun* began its journey—are left with awe at their discoveries, unanswerable questions, and no chance of establishing contact with this intelligent extraterrestrial life. Still, the discovery has been made. Humankind is not alone in the universe.

A Profound Impact

The story of Darwin IV, Leo, and Ike may not be real, but, says scientist J. Craig Venter, who mapped the human genome, "I think discovering life on another planet might be one of the most fantastic things for humans."[3] Although such a discovery would inevitably have a profound impact on humanity, other scientists are not so sure that it would be desirable. Leo and Ike illustrate just one way that encountering extraterrestrial life could be dangerous. Communication efforts may falter, and robot or human explorers might be attacked through misunderstandings.

Scientists surmise that extraterrestrial life could pose a danger to human beings in several ways, whether humankind is exploring space or staying home. Exploration might expose humans to one kind of threat, but avoiding exploration may not be a safe strategy either. Earthlings may not need to send robots to distant planets to find aliens. Extraterrestrial life might find us.

CHAPTER ONE

Is Any Kind of Life Out There?

In his Foundation series, the late science-fiction writer and biochemist Isaac Asimov imagined a Milky Way galaxy devoid of any alien sentient life and thinly populated by lower life-forms of little meaning or threat to the humans colonizing the Earthlike planets in the galaxy. Not until he hinted at the possibility of intergalactic threat, thousands of years in the future he imagined, did Asimov consider contact between humans and other intelligent life. And then, he hinted at an ominous threat to the very existence of humanity.

The late astrophysicist and writer Carl Sagan, however, in his science-fiction book *Contact*, imagines a different kind of galaxy altogether—one in which humans in the near future make contact with advanced beings who are as curious and questioning as humans and want to peacefully exchange knowledge and ideas. Different scientists, philosophers, and writers have imagined many ways to answer the question: Does life exist in the universe anywhere but on Earth, and what kind might it be?

Life: A Miracle or Inevitable?

Wondering about what alien life might be like requires the basic assumption that life arose somewhere besides on Earth. Despite much speculation, no one has been able to scientifically prove that humans share the universe with life of any kind, let alone intelligent aliens that might be a threat to humanity. Some scientists consider the existence of extraterrestrial life to be unlikely, if only because they see the rise of life on Earth as a freak occurrence. Francis Crick, for example, who is the codiscoverer of the structure of DNA, says, "The origin of life appears at the moment to be almost a miracle, so many are the conditions which would have had to have been satisfied to get it going."[4] Physicist and astrobiologist Paul Davies agrees that life looks almost like "magic" and may or may not be impossibly rare. Chemist George Whitesides has written, "How remarkable is life? The answer is: *very*. Those of us who deal in networks of chemical reactions know of nothing like it. . . . How could a chemical sludge become a rose, even with billions of years to try? . . . It is not impossible, but it seems very, very improbable."[5] If life is almost a miracle, then perhaps no extraterrestrial life exists, and humans are alone in the universe.

Many, if not most, other scientists, however, do believe that extraterrestrial life is likely to exist. They suggest that the evolution of life is almost inevitable given the right conditions and a likely planet. They often argue that to assume Earth is the only place in the vast universe where life has arisen is ridiculous. While they have no proof, they do have tantalizing evidence and logic on their side. Physicist Stephen Hawking, for example, argues, "One piece of evidence that suggests the probability of primitive forms of life appearing may be reasonably high is that life seems to have appeared on Earth shortly after the Earth cooled sufficiently for life to be possible. If life was very unlikely, one might have expected life not to have appeared until late in the 10 billion years or so that the Earth has to live."[6]

Renowned British physicist Stephen Hawking, lecturing on his research in 2010, does not believe that Earth is the only inhabited planet in the universe. He has also stated publicly that extraterrestrial life may represent a threat to Earth's inhabitants.

Life appeared on Earth, scientists say, about 3.5 to 4 billion years ago, and the planet is only about 4.5 billion years old—not even halfway through its time span. Hawking can imagine life to be not an improbable event but perhaps a likely one because it arose on Earth so quickly, in terms of geological time. The discovery of even primitive life-forms on other planets might prove which point of view is correct.

Alien Life in the Solar System

The search for signs of life anywhere in Earth's solar system or outside it is a major goal of the National Aeronautics and Space Administration (NASA). NASA's Astrobiology Program is dedicated to answering three fundamental questions: "How does life begin and evolve? Is there life beyond Earth and, if so, how can we detect it? What is the future of life on Earth and in the universe?"[7]

NASA scientists of the Astrobiology Program conduct an ongoing search within the solar system for evidence that primitive, microscopic living organisms, or microbes, such as bacteria or viruses or fungi, ever evolved on Mars or other planets. If such microbes exist now or ever existed in the past, scientists would have evidence that life also evolved somewhere other than on Earth and perhaps that life is a common occurrence rather than a unique, special circumstance of Earth. Since scientists believe that all life evolves from single-celled microbes, finding microbial life would be evidence that higher alien life-forms are possible.

On Mars, scientific exploration with robots and probes concentrates on the strategy "follow the water" because scientists believe that water is necessary for life to arise. They try to identify habitable zones—suitable places on Mars where conditions are such that life is at least possible. NASA says,

> Following the water begins with an understanding of the current environment on Mars. We want to explore observed features like dry riverbeds, ice in the polar caps and rock types that only form when water is present. We want to look for hot springs, hydrothermal vents or subsurface water reserves. We want to understand if ancient Mars once held a vast ocean in the northern hemisphere as some scientists believe.[8]

The Tantalizing Evidence

In 2008 NASA's *Phoenix* Mars lander spent five months analyzing the icy soil of Mars's northern polar region before the lander froze in the cold of the Martian winter. *Phoenix* confirmed the presence of patches of underground water ice. It discovered a mineral, calcium carbonate, which may indicate occasional presence of thawed water. It observed falling snow. And, perhaps most interestingly, it discovered a chemical called perchlorate that is a food for some microbes on Earth. None of this is proof of life on Mars, but lead mission scientist Peter Smith of the University of Arizona in Tucson says, "We found that the soil above the ice can act like a sponge, with perchlorate scavenging water from the atmosphere and holding on to it. You can have a thin film layer of water capable of being a habitable environment. A micro-world at the scale of grains of soil—that's where the action is."[9]

In the future, NASA along with other space agencies around the world hopes to launch a complex robotic mission—the Mars Science Laboratory. It will analyze Martian soil and rocks for evidence of the organic

Life on Enceladus?

Enceladus is a small, icy moon orbiting Saturn. Its surface is frozen, with temperatures about -324°F (-197.8°C). It seems to be an unlikely place for life to develop, but since 2005 NASA's spacecraft Cassini has flown by the moon several times and recorded the presence of spewing salt water, warm fissures in the ice with temperatures of -120ºF (-84.4ºC), and chemical elements such as carbon, hydrogen, oxygen, potassium, and nitrogen. The plumes also contain ammonia, which can act like antifreeze. NASA scientist Dennis Matson says that the source of all these phenomena must be a liquid ocean under the moon's icy crust. Enceladus seems to have the major ingredients necessary for life—liquid water, organic compounds, and heat. Cassini will continue to explore Saturn's moons until 2017, and no one knows what else it might find. But scientists are excited by the idea that someday they may find alien microbial life on Enceladus.

compounds necessary for life. It will also analyze the soil for water and other indications that Mars is now or once was able to provide a habitat for microbial life.

Steven Squyres, an astronomer and lead scientist with NASA's Mars exploration missions, is convinced that at least at one time Mars had an environment that could support life. Two Martian rovers, *Spirit* and *Opportunity*, have found evidence of past surface water, minerals that form in the presence of water, and hot springs that could have produced steam.

Within the sulfur-rich soil of Mars (pictured in this image taken by the NASA exploration rover Spirit*) may lie microbial life-forms that have adjusted to the planet's harsh environment.*

Squyres says, "When you have the evidence right there in front of you for habitability, it makes a convincing case that you [had] better go out and see if anyone lived out there."[10]

Squyres does not mean that intelligent life ever existed on Mars, but even the discovery of microbial life elsewhere in the solar system would be profoundly exciting to scientists. If scientists can find solid evidence that microbes lived on Mars in the past, some scientists argue that their descendants could still be alive today. Underground on Mars, liquid water and warmth might still exist and so might alien life. On Earth, microbes live in the most extreme of places, deep inside rock fissures and never exposed to the sun. They live in habitats that are extremely cold and extremely hot. Logically, such life could exist on Mars as well. The search for this microbial life, says Phoenix mission scientist Carol Stoker, should include future missions capable of drilling into Martian soil to look for life-forms that have adjusted to Mars's harsh environment. She says that Mars may still have habitable zones where life exists.

Is Europa the Jackpot?

NASA researchers and other scientists see the potential for habitable zones in other parts of the solar system, too. Perhaps, say some scientists, the life-forms may be more complex than microbes. Europa, one of the planet Jupiter's moons, is covered in ice that is 50 to 100 miles (80 to 160 km) thick. Underneath this ice, scientists believe, is a liquid ocean. NASA and the European Space Agency (ESA) plan a mission to Europa and neighboring moons of Jupiter in 2020 to search for information about the possibility that this ocean could be a habitable home for living things. Scientists have evidence that Europa's ocean has tides, salt, and oxygen, all of which could make the environment hospitable to life.

Frank Drake and the Drake Equation

Frank Drake is considered the father of SETI and conducted the first SETI search in 1960. He used a radio telescope in West Virginia to search the skies for radio waves from an extraterrestrial intelligence. In 1961 he developed a mathematical tool for estimating the number of advanced civilizations in the galaxy. The formula is called the Drake Equation. The factors of the equation are:

1. The rate of formation of types of stars in the Milky Way that could support life.
2. The fraction of those stars with planet systems.
3. The number of planets in each solar system that are Earthlike or suitable for life.
4. The fraction of Earthlike planets upon which life appears.
5. The fraction of those planets where intelligent life evolves.
6. The fraction of those planets that develop a technological civilization.
7. The average length of time that civilizations emit radio waves.

The only factor that is known to scientists is number 1. All the other factors are unknown, and different scientists make different guesses about them. The Drake equation has no solution. It is simply a tool for scientists to try to estimate the number of technological civilizations that might exist today. Using the Drake Equation, many scientists have come up with many different estimates of the number of advanced civilizations in the Milky Way, from 1 (Earth's) to 10,000 to millions.

At the University of Arizona, professor of planetary sciences Richard Greenberg studies Europa and believes that it presents the best chance of finding life in the solar system. He says, "There is nothing saying there is life there now. But we do know that there are the physical conditions to support it."[11] Greenberg has calculated that conditions could support not just microorganisms but also as much as 3 tons (2.7 metric tons) of multicellular organisms or animals such as fishlike creatures. On the basis of his study of Earth's deep seas, scientist Timothy Shank says that he would be surprised if life does not exist on Europa.

Scientists imagine that someday they will be able to send probes to Europa that will bore through the ice crust and search the ocean below for life. Although that idea is far in the future, NASA scientist Robert Pappalardo says, "Icy moons may be the most common habitats for life in the Universe, so studying Europa will help tell us not just whether life exists elsewhere in our Solar System, but how common life may be throughout the Universe."[12]

Life Outside the Solar System

Even if no alien life exists in Earth's solar system, life still may be common in other star systems in the galaxy. The search for extrasolar planets—planets outside Earth's solar system—capable of supporting life is the goal of NASA's Kepler telescope mission. The orbiting spacecraft's telescope is trained on a small portion of the Milky Way galaxy and searches for signs of planets around some 100,000 stars. It finds possible planets by measuring the extremely tiny dimming of a star's light when a planet crosses in front of the star. With the Kepler telescope, scientists have identified gas giants (planets like Jupiter), ice giants, and very hot super-Earths that are large and orbiting close to their stars.

Finding small, rocky planets the size of Earth, however, is difficult, just because they are so small and would take a relatively long time to orbit their stars. So far, although Kepler has found more than 700 possible planets, NASA scientists have not yet confirmed that any are Earthlike or in the right kind of orbit to support life. Scientists say that for life to develop, a planet must be in the "Goldilocks Zone"[13] of a star. This

> **DID YOU KNOW?**
>
> The Kepler telescope mission is named in honor of sixteenth-century astronomer Johannes Kepler, who thought that creatures like reptiles lived on the moon.

means an orbit similar to Earth's—not too close and not too far away from its star; not too hot and not too cold; just right for there to be liquid water. Kepler has to collect about three years' worth of data about planets orbiting stars in order to confirm the presence of an Earthlike planet in a Goldilocks Zone. Many scientists expect, however, to find that the galaxy is rich in Earthlike planets.

In September 2010 in Hawaii, a team of scientists used a different way to measure the presence of a planet with the Keck telescope and found the first known planet in the Goldilocks Zone, named Gliese 581g. Astronomer Seth Shostak says, "Several decades ago we didn't even know if most solar systems had planets. Now we have already spotted more than 400 extrasolar planets, and we are finding more all the time. If we find out that 3% of all solar systems have terrestrial planets, then there should be 10 billion earthlike worlds in the galaxy."[14]

The Search for Intelligent Life

No one is sure that Earthlike worlds support alien life, let alone intelligent life, but Shostak believes in the likelihood of intelligent extraterrestrial life, too. He explains that with so many Earthlike planets in the galaxy, intelligent life does not have to evolve very often for it to exist on many worlds. He says, "Even assuming that only one in a million of these planets harbors intelligent life, that still leaves 10,000 civilizations."[15]

Shostak is the senior astronomer at the SETI Institute in California. SETI is the Search for Extraterrestrial Intelligence. The SETI Institute is a private, nonprofit organization of about 150 scientists and other staff working at three centers in California. The community of SETI scientists partners with other astronomy research centers around the world and uses their radio telescope arrays and antennae to conduct searches for signs of radio communications from intelligent life in the galaxy. SETI scientists have conducted more than 100 listening projects when the telescopes are not needed for other astronomy research. For example, the SETI Institute used the Arecibo Observatory telescope in Puerto Rico and the Parkes telescope in Australia for listening projects. Also, in 2007, with the University of California at Berkeley, the SETI Institute built the Allen Telescope Array in California so that it can search the heavens for radio waves on a full-time basis. The SETI Mission statement says, "We believe we are conducting the most profound search in human history."[16]

The SETI Institute, as yet, has identified no signal from the stars that can be interpreted as coming from an alien intelligence. Nevertheless, scientists such as Shostak are far from discouraged. The institute continually searches for purposeful messages that an alien intelligence might be sending in the direction of Earth. And it searches for "accidental" signals or the radio noise that could leak into space from a civilization with advanced technology. Even with years spent searching, it has carefully examined only about 1,000 stars out of billions. Shostak says, "We are looking for a needle in a haystack. . . . We know how big the haystack is—it's the galaxy. We don't know how many needles there are, but we can reckon how fast we're going through the hay."[17]

With its new and advanced telescope array, the SETI Institute is searching at an ever increasing rate. Shostak insists that finding an "ET" message is not too far in the future. Different scientists have suggested different estimations of the number of intelligent civilizations in the galaxy. Shostak explains:

Carl Sagan figured a couple of million [advanced civilizations], and if he's right we should succeed by 2015. Isaac Asimov figured 670,000, and if he's right, it should take until 2023. Frank Drake [the founder of SETI] is more conservative, with only 10,000 civilizations broadcasting in the galaxy right now, and consequently it takes until 2027. . . . Mind you, all of these numbers could be completely wrong, but it is these guesses that motivate our efforts.[18]

A habitable liquid ocean might exist beneath the icy surface of Europa, one of Jupiter's moons. A color-enhanced image of Europa taken by the Galileo *spacecraft shows ice contaminated with rocky material (red or brown); fine-grained ice (light blue); coarse-grained ice (dark blue); and cracks in the icy crust (brown lines).*

Does SETI Make Sense?

During his lifetime, Sagan argued strongly in favor of the SETI mission because he believed that extraterrestrial civilizations are almost sure to exist. In a 1978 article, he wrote, "Personally, I think it far more difficult to understand a universe in which we are the only technological civilization, or one of but a few, than to imagine a cosmos brimming over with intelligent life."[19] Many scientists, writers, and others have agreed with Sagan. The science-fiction writer Arthur C. Clarke, whose novel *2001: A Space Odyssey* was later made into a movie, once said, "The idea that we are the only intelligent creatures in a cosmos of a hundred billion galaxies is so preposterous that there are very few astronomers today who would take it seriously."[20]

Not every scientist agrees that the galaxy must be swarming with intelligent life. Some echo the physicist Enrico Fermi's famous question. Fermi not only worked on the development of the first atomic bomb but also was considered a genius because of his contributions to the sciences of physics and astrophysics. One day in 1950 he and a group of fellow physicists were discussing the probability of extraterrestrial life. Fermi's response to those who argued that such life was likely was, "So? Where is everybody?"[21] Fermi meant that if the galaxy is full of billions of Earth-like planets and if millions of intelligent civilizations exist, Earth should already have been found and visited by extraterrestrials. Since no scientific evidence of any visits has been found, to assume that extraterrestrial civilizations exist is not logical.

Fermi's question has become known as Fermi's paradox. The paradox is the contradiction between the idea that intelligent aliens are common and Earth's lack of contact with them. The lack of contact is especially meaningful because planets at the center of the galaxy formed millions of years before Earth did. So, civilizations far in advance of Earth's and capable of space travel should have developed long ago. Yet humanity has not been contacted by any intelligent aliens. The simplest answer to the paradox is that intelligent extraterrestrial life does not exist.

Physicist Michio Kaku, however, argues against the simple answer. He says:

> Recently some astronomers have said Bah, humbug! The conditions for life are extremely rare. For example, you need a large moon to stabilize the orbit of the Earth or else the Earth tumbles in its orbit. You need a large Jupiter to clean out the comets and meteors of the solar system. You have to have so many Goldilocks Zones. The Earth has to be just right for this, just right for that that perhaps we are alone. Well, I don't think so. 'Cause if you look at the number of stars in the heavens, perhaps 10 billion trillion stars that are within the range of our telescopes, and you realize that half of them, perhaps half of them have solar systems around them. And if you play the odds, you come up with the realization that perhaps there are billions, billions of planets in our universe that have conditions that are compatible with life as we know it.[22]

So Should Earth Get Ready?

Davies believes that life may be common in the universe. "However," he says, "we must never allow speculation to replace real science." As yet, no real science proves the existence of other life in the galaxy, whether primitive or intelligent. Says Davies, "It could be that life is common, but intelligence is rare."[23] That is why Davies named his book about the search for alien life *The Eerie Silence*. If intelligent extraterrestrial beings exist, why have humans never heard from them? Perhaps, he speculates, interstellar distances are too great, not only for traveling between the stars but even for a message. Perhaps intelligent life exists, but it did not discover science and cannot communicate with other planets. Perhaps all intelligent civilizations are doomed to destroy themselves, and extraterrestrial civilizations died out before earthlings developed technology. Perhaps they simply have not discovered Earth yet.

Amidst the speculation about the existence of extraterrestrial life, scientists ponder another important question: If extraterrestrial life is out there, does humanity want to risk finding it? Would any kind of extraterrestrial contact—whether intelligent or microscopic and primitive—pose a threat to Earth and to humankind?

CHAPTER TWO

The Threat from Microscopic Life

After Neil Armstrong and Buzz Aldrin made their historic walk on the moon during NASA's Apollo 11 Mission in 1969, they climbed back into the *Eagle* lunar module and discovered that not only their spacesuits and helmets but also their bodies were covered with lunar dust. They were as prepared as possible for this eventuality. Each man brushed and vacuumed the other and then the whole interior of the lunar module. They cleaned themselves with tissues and towels soaked in hot water. They used the vacuum tool to blow any dust into the air filters of the module. The sticky lunar dust would not come completely out from under their fingernails, but they did the best they could.

When they returned to Earth on July 24, the astronauts landed in the ocean, where navy frogman Clancy Hatleberg swam up to their capsule, opened the hatch, and handed them isolation suits to wear. As they crawled out of the capsule, the frogman sprayed them with disinfectant. Only then could the astronauts climb aboard the waiting life raft. In the raft, they cleaned themselves with cloths and chemical detergent. Hatleberg tied the cloths to weights and then threw them into the ocean. Once the astronauts got to the navy ship assigned to recovering them, they walked immediately to an isolation trailer on the ship and stayed there until the trailer was transported by plane and truck to the Lunar

Receiving Laboratory in Houston. There, the astronauts were isolated and quarantined until August 10 in an effort to ensure that no trace of lunar material they might carry could infect Earth. They, their equipment, and any other people exposed to them were medically checked and rechecked. The gear and lunar samples they brought home with them were examined for microbial growth in NASA laboratories. Mice were injected with lunar material and watched for signs of any reaction. All of these precautions were based on NASA's fear that lunar microbes might be unleashed on Earth and cause terrible epidemics of alien disease.

Microbes Can Survive

Even in 1969, remembers William Carpentier, the flight surgeon in charge, scientists did not really believe that "moon bugs" existed or could infect Earth. They were almost certain that the moon was a sterile world with no life. But Carpentier explains, "We just couldn't take the risk."[24]

The moon is a lifeless world, but the idea of extraterrestrial microbial life that might endanger Earth is not far-fetched. If any microbes do live on Mars, for instance, or in other places in the solar system, they could be very hardy forms of life. Alien microbes might well be able to hitch a ride on a spacecraft or probe, survive the trip through space, and then infect Earth once the mission returned home.

Scientists know that Earth microbes can survive in space. For example, the European Space Agency collected bacterial spores from rocks near Beer, England, and placed them on and in small pieces of limestone. These rocks were sent to the International Space Station and placed on the outside of the station. They were exposed to the vacuum of space, deadly ultraviolet rays from the sun, and extremely cold temperatures.

After 533 days, some of those spores were still alive. In 2010 colonies of bacteria grown from those spores continued to thrive in a laboratory in England.

In 1967 the *Surveyor 3*, a probe sent to the moon, carried a camera accidentally contaminated with about 50 to 100 streptococcus bacteria. Apparently, the camera had been contaminated by someone who handled it on Earth. The bacteria survived the rocket liftoff and the trip to the moon. They survived the lunar landing and the airless surface of the moon. They remained dormant, unable to grow or reproduce, and without water or nutrients—but still living—for almost three years. Then, the astronauts of the Apollo 12 mission landed on the moon near *Surveyor 3* and retrieved the camera to take back to NASA scientists. That was when the bacteria were discovered. They were still alive and able to grow

Apollo 11 *astronauts (from left to right) Neil Armstrong, Michael Collins, and Buzz Aldrin greet President Richard Nixon from inside an isolation chamber after their successful 1969 journey to the moon. The astronauts were isolated and quarantined to prevent a possible lunar infection on Earth.*

and reproduce in NASA labs. Apollo 12 astronaut Pete Conrad said, "I have always thought the most significant thing that we ever found on the whole . . . Moon was that little bacteria who came back and lived."[25]

Is Earth Already Threatened?

The extreme hardiness of bacteria and viruses has led some scientists to theorize that microorganisms can live in comets and meteors and travel through space for hundreds of years before reaching planets where, if conditions are suitable, they can flourish and grow. Two astronomers, Chandra Wickramasinghe and Fred Hoyle, have argued that life on Earth began because microbes from space seeded the planet millions of years ago. The theory is called *panspermia*. According to this theory, microorganisms or their spores could have seeded the atmosphere when Earth passed through the tail of a comet, or they could have fallen to Earth in a meteorite. Once established on Earth, the microbes grew and evolved, and life began.

Microbes such as bacteria and viruses commonly mutate, meaning their genes change as they reproduce, and they become new forms of microorganisms. Some of these microorganisms can infect humans with diseases to which they have no resistance. Most scientists today reject panspermia as an unsubstantiated theory, but Wickramasinghe and a few others take the idea of microbes traveling to Earth even further. They theorize that some epidemics and plagues throughout Earth's history may have been caused by microbes from space.

> ### DID YOU KNOW?
>
> In 2003 the space probe *Galileo* was at the end of its Jupiter mission, so NASA scientists intentionally crashed it into Jupiter to protect the moon Europa from any contamination by Earth germs.

Death from the Skies

Plague is caused by a bacterium that is anaerobic—it survives without oxygen—and it can live in freezing cold temperatures. Since space is co'

Guarding Mars

Planetary Protection Officer Catharine Conley has identified the special regions on Mars where the dangers of Earth contamination are of greatest concern. These areas include any known feature that suggests the presence of liquid water. For example, gullies, channels, and fresh craters are special regions. "Pasted-on terrain" is a special region where smooth material, such as snow or ice, lies on top of permanent terrain, such as rock. Any area that is 16 feet (5 m) or more beneath the Martian surface is also a special region. Space probes that land in or drill into a special region are in an area where Earth microbes have the best chance of surviving and growing. They are also operating in areas where the best chance of Martian microbes exists.

Therefore, all such probes must be cleaned, heat baked, and assembled in sterile environments. No probe can be made completely sterile without destroying the probe itself, so planetary protection protocols for special regions set a limit of the fewest and most weakened microbes possible. Today, this means mathematically determining that for the next 40 years the chance of infecting Mars is less than 0.01 percent.

and has no oxygen, Wickramasinghe asks, "Therefore, could these microbes have originated in space?"[26] He wonders if the microbes were first in Earth's atmosphere, were bombarded and mutated by the sun's radiation, and then fell onto Earth where they infected animals. He looks at the way the plague called the Black Death spread in Europe from 1334 to 1350 and says it did not follow the route that people traveled from place to place. Instead, it traveled a route as if carried by the winds.

When a comet travels near the sun, the solar winds and radiation hit the comet and blast its surfaces. This causes a tail of particles and dust to form that can be millions of miles long. It can cause shooting stars and small meteorites to break off of the comet and fall to Earth. In this debris, says Wickramasinghe, microbes could survive. They could float in the upper atmosphere for years and perhaps infect birds or flying insects. They could travel in Earth's jet streams and then slowly drift downward. Perhaps, he argues, this is how influenza epidemics caused by viruses are born.

Comets come close to Earth with regularity. In 1908 Comet Encke came extremely close to Earth and passed again in 1914. Both times, Wickramasinghe explains, it shed ice, rocks, and dust into Earth's atmosphere. In 1918 the world experienced a pandemic of influenza that killed or sickened 100 million people. Wickramasinghe says, "There is as yet no way to determine if a comet played a role in the plague of 1918. However, it is now known that this epidemic began in birds which were the first to die, infected with some mysterious disease that fell from the sky."[27] Comet Encke approached Earth closely again in 2007, and Wickramasinghe wonders if the new influenza virus H1N1, or swine flu, that caused another pandemic in 2009 came from space and the comet.

Wickramasinghe's speculations are not supported by any evidence. He himself admits, "Correlation is not causation and thus no firm conclusions can be drawn, despite the wealth of evidence suggesting a link between comets and diseases from space."[28] Just because two things happen at the same time does not mean that one caused the other. However, the threat of alien microbes causing deadly diseases is real to many scientists.

The Microbial Threat of Space Exploration

Just as NASA scientists once feared the threat of moon microbes, some worry about the threat of possible Mars germs. So far, all the probes sent from Earth to Mars have remained on Mars, exploring and collecting samples and sending the data back. However, in the future, NASA plans Mars missions that will collect Martian samples and then return, with the samples, to Earth. And someday, humans will travel to Mars. Scientist Jeffrey Kargel warns, "Before proceeding with sample returns or human missions to Mars, we must review measures for planetary biological protection."[29]

If microbes do live on Mars and are inadvertently brought back to Earth, no one knows how they might affect life on Earth. Even if such microbes cannot infect humans and cause dangerous diseases, they still might survive and flourish here and perhaps change the natural environment, or biosphere, forever. Kargel suggests that a future human mission to Mars that results in confirmed microbial contamination might mean that the astronauts would have to stay on Mars the rest of their lives in order to protect Earth.

A worst-case scenario of extraterrestrial microbes invading Earth was imagined in the 1969 novel *The Andromeda Strain*, written by Michael Crichton. In the story, the alien microbes travel to Earth on a returning space satellite that was hit by a meteor as it orbited Earth. A deadly microbe from the meteor infects people, killing them by turning their blood to powder within seconds. Even though *The Andromeda Strain* is fiction, the idea of dangerous extraterrestrial microbes is not necessarily a fantasy. Microbiologist Abigail A. Salyers says that while the story is "wildly improbable," extraterrestrial microbes, if they exist, might possibly be able to infect humans. She explains:

> **DID YOU KNOW?**
> Extremophiles are microbes that can live and thrive in conditions that would kill most life. Earth's extremophiles are indirect evidence that extraterrestrial microbes could exist.

> Could a microbe that evolved in a place where there are no humans possibly cause infection in humans? From our experience here on Earth, we know that the answer to this question is Yes. There have been many examples of human infections caused by bacteria or viruses that have come out of soil or water, locations where they had not had much or any prior contact with humans, or that were previously known to infect only nonhuman animals. Examples are Legionnaire's disease, a lung infection caused by a bacterium that normally resides in water, and AIDS, a viral infection that probably originated in monkeys and later jumped to humans who were hunting and eating monkeys.[30]

Technicians deliver a box containing moon rock samples to scientists in Houston, Texas. NASA examined samples such as these for microbial growth.

Salyers does not believe that alien microbes would be likely to infect humans, however. She points out that any bacteria or viruses that evolved on, for example, Mars or Europa would be suited to very cold temperatures. They would probably grow poorly or die in the warm human body. A group of scientists with the National Research Council agrees that the probability that alien microbes could contaminate Earth is extremely low. The scientists explain that most microorganisms on Earth are benign—they do not cause disease in humans or animals. Alien microbes would be even less likely to have evolved to the point of being able to infect people or animals on Earth. They would likely be unable to survive and grow on Earth at all or to compete with Earth's own microbes. "However," state the scientists, "any assessment of the potential for harmful effects involves many uncertainties, and the risk is not zero."[31]

Protecting Earth from Aliens

Because the risk is not zero, every country that has a space program has signed an international treaty that requires a planetary protection officer to guard against Earth's contamination with alien life-forms. One of NASA's first planetary protection officers was John Rummel. He once explained, "If there's something alive out there, we don't want to bring it back and spread it around without knowing something about it."[32] Rummel admits that no one really expects an Andromeda strain if NASA brings extraterrestrial samples back to Earth, but he and other scientists still believe in the importance of safety from the unknown and unexpected.

In his role as planetary protection officer, Rummel helped NASA develop regulations to carefully contain any material or samples in secure, sealed containers before it is brought back to Earth from any space missions that involve contact with a solar system body. Even on Earth-orbiting space stations, such as the International Space Station, microbes from Earth can find warm, wet, undisturbed corners in which to exist and multiply. Although such microbes might carry disease, they are not

A Symphony of Scientists

In 2010 a musical project called Symphony of Science released "The Case for Mars," a music video (which can be seen on YouTube) about the importance of human exploration of Mars. Four scientists are featured in the music video. They are not afraid of Mars microbes or the dangers of exploring a new planet. Instead, they sing about how exciting visiting Mars would be. The late Carl Sagan describes the amazing features of Mars—its volcanoes, its great rift valley—and sings "Mars is a world of wonders." Aerospace engineer Robert Zubrin describes its habitability—its water, carbon, and the warmth in its interior; he insists that contamination is a "dragon" people can slay instead of fear. Astrobiologist Penelope Boston points out how similar ancient Mars was to ancient Earth; she strongly believes that Mars could be a home to alien microbes. Physicist Brian Cox sings about its river valleys and ice sheets and about how Mars is "a dry, frozen version of our own home." These scientists urge the world to envision a future for humanity that includes expansion of the human race to Mars.

Robert Zubrin et al., "The Case for Mars," Symphony of Science, video. www.symphonyof
science.com.

alien and therefore would not threaten Earth with extraterrestrial contamination.

Rummel's job is to plan for unmanned missions to alien solar system bodies, such as moons, planets, comets, and asteroids. If the mission involves a return to Earth with a sample from the body, scientists have to be absolutely sure that it does not carry any microscopic hitchhiker that might threaten Earth. Rummel helped NASA build a containment laboratory where the samples can be safely studied. If a returning probe is not certain to be free of contamination, Rummel's plans include sterilizing the probe before it reaches Earth or destroying it before it can return.

Preventing the Spread of Earth Germs

NASA's current planetary protection officer is Catharine Conley, who says of her job, "The highest priority is to prevent contamination of the Earth."[33] But, as yet, no probe that might harbor life-forms has been brought back to Earth. Protecting Earth from extraterrestrial contamination is a future problem, not a current one. Conley has to prepare for these predicted future missions, but today she has another important job. She must help protect the solar system from the threat of contamination by Earth. Rummel calls it "saving the universe from the scum of the Earth."[34]

NASA's Planetary Protection website explains that its goal is protection for "all of the planets, all of the time." It states, "Our mission is to prevent biological cross-contamination that could result from NASA's solar system exploration missions."[35] No one is sure that Earth's microbes could survive and grow elsewhere in the solar system. The Earth microbes that survived on the moon did not establish a moon colony. However, other bodies in the solar system might be more hospitable to microorganisms. Conley does not want to risk contaminating these places in the solar system with alien Earth microorganisms. In an educational presentation, she warns that Earth must not "spill" the "primordial soup"[36] (the primitive beginnings of life) into alien environments.

Planetary Protection regulations assign each NASA mission to a category. Category I mission destinations do not require special protection from Earth contamination. For example, the moon, Mercury, and the sun are in Category I because life as scientists understand it could not be sustained in those places. Any mission to a solar system body where the possibility of life is believed to be remote is a Category II mission. Venus would be in this category. Category III is reserved for missions with spacecraft that orbit or fly by a body where life is possible. Category IV is for a mission that actually lands where life is possible. Mars, the moons of Jupiter, and the moons of Saturn are in Category IV. The higher the category, the more carefully NASA scientists work to make the mission probe or robot clean and sterile before it leaves Earth.

All NASA's spacecraft destined for Mars landings, for example, are built in special clean rooms by people wearing protective clothing such as surgical masks, booties, and gloves. The environment is kept as sterile as possible, and before launch, the spacecraft is decontaminated by being baked in dry heat. Larry Esposito, a University of Colorado professor of planetary sciences explains, "We're concerned about life everywhere, and we don't want to pollute or invade other locations with Earth life."[37]

However, baking is not the same as complete sterilization, and some scientists worry that Mars is already contaminated by Earth microbes from the Viking landers that were sent there in the 1970s. Others believe that the environment of Mars is too harsh for Earth microorganisms to survive for long, even if they did hitch a ride on a spacecraft. NASA Planetary Protection continues to research ways to make its spacecraft 100 percent sterile, just to be absolutely certain that future missions to Mars and elsewhere do not infect other places in the solar system.

Doing the Right Thing

"Should we care if we spread Earth life to other planets in our solar system, or anywhere else?"[38] asks science writer Laura Woodmansee. Rummel answers that Earth's inhabitants should care, and for important scientific reasons. He says infecting another planet or moon in the solar system with Earth life might harm or kill any life already there. Or in the search for alien life, scientists might mistake hitchhiking Earth life for alien life. Rummel explains why the planetary protection policy matters. He says, "The policy is actually based on the desire to preserve extraterrestrial environments for the science opportunities that are there.

It's in nobody's best interest to obscure that by contamination with Earth organisms. Nor would you want to discover a wonderful new life form and know that you've killed it. . . . Essentially we can meet ethical considerations by the desire to preserve science."[39] Contaminating an alien environment with Earth life would make the search for extraterrestrial life much harder than it already is.

SETI Institute scientists Margaret S. Race and Richard O. Randolph also argue that for Earth to endanger primitive extraterrestrial life would be as unethical as to threaten intelligent alien life. They say that humans have the same moral responsibility to care about extraterrestrial ecosystems as they do to protect Earth. Such ecosystems deserve the right to develop naturally and not be destroyed by human explorers. The scientists explain, "If planet Earth were visited by extraterrestrial beings with vastly superior intellectual capacities, we would want them to respect the Earth's life, ecosystems and evolutionary trajectory, or at least not interfere in harmful ways. Similarly, we should follow the same ethical considerations when human explorers play the role of the intellectually superior species vis-a-vis non-intelligent ET life."[40]

> ### DID YOU KNOW?
>
> NASA's Stardust mission collected a sample of particles from a comet and returned them to Earth in a capsule inside a contamination-free container in 2006.

The Lesson of Earth History

Even though no microbial life has been found anywhere but on Earth, scientists do believe that microbial life is the most likely and abundant form of life in the galaxy. If they are correct, then humans must be concerned about both the threat Earth might pose to alien microbial life and the threat that alien microbial life might pose to Earth. Some scientists argue that if Earth were ever visited by intelligent life, the danger would not be from them but from the germs they carry with them. Physicist and mathematician B.G. Sidharth says,

When Columbus was followed by the Spanish conquistadors, it was not advanced weaponry which destroyed the native civilizations, but disease. The Spanish soldiers and monks carried diseases the natives had never before encountered and they died in vast numbers. Therefore it could be argued that the greatest threat is not from alien conquistadors. It is exposure to alien microorganisms which might prove disastrous to the inhabitants of Earth.[41]

And the danger might be mutual.

CHAPTER THREE

The Threat from Intelligent Extraterrestrials

If intelligent extraterrestrial life exists, could it be a threat to humanity? Perhaps advanced, intelligent aliens could hatch a plan to conquer Earth without ever leaving home by using microbes as their weapons of choice. Chandra Wickramasinghe imagines an extraterrestrial civilization living somewhere in the galaxy and facing extinction on its own planet. Perhaps war has made the planet unlivable, or perhaps its sun is dying. For whatever reason, the aliens need a way to preserve something of themselves. Wickramasinghe says the civilization "may well decide to package its genetic heritage within microbes, including viruses, and launch them out into space."[42] They would not even need space rockets; they could seed comets with the viruses that carried their genes. Maybe most of the microbes would die, but some could land on habitable planets and become the beginnings of a kind of colonization by the alien culture. The microbes carrying their genes might begin the process of evolution and ensure that the extraterrestrial life-forms continued. Some of these microbes, however, might reach Earth, and if they did, they could cause terrible, untreatable diseases.

Wickramasinghe believes such a scenario could be even more dangerous to earthlings than the plagues and epidemics that he posits are arriving accidentally on comets and meteors. He says, "The aliens we have to fear are not superintelligent creatures arriving in space ships and intending to conquer and subdue us, but sub-micron sized viral invaders that may threaten the very existence of our species."[43]

Other people have imagined even more sinister situations. On the website Weird Sciences, for example, a physics and engineering student suggests the possibility of a predatory alien culture using viruses as weapons against humans. The viruses would be sent to Earth where they would infect people, penetrate their cells, and cause changes in human DNA that could wipe out the people of Earth. Then, the aliens could take over Earth without risking a fight with its human residents.

Stephen Hawking's Threatening Aliens

Of course, no one knows if intelligent aliens exist, much less whether they would be friendly or threatening to Earth's inhabitants. Stephen Hawking, a scientist who specializes in physics and cosmology (the study of the nature of the universe), has been called the smartest man living in the world today. Because of the size of the galaxy and the likelihood of multitudes of habitable planets, he says, "To my mathematical brain, the numbers alone make thinking about aliens perfectly rational." Hawking has thought about the probability that intelligent extraterrestrials almost certainly exist and explains, "The real challenge is to work out what aliens might actually be like."[44]

In his 2010 Discovery Channel television series *Into the Universe with Stephen Hawking* Hawking presents his ideas about what intelligent aliens might be like, and his thoughts are frightening. He warns that intelligent extraterrestrials might not be as friendly as people hope. Hawking envisions a highly advanced space-traveling civilization that could be very danger-

> **DID YOU KNOW?**
> The US Air Force investigated reports of unidentified flying objects from 1947 to 1969 and concluded that no evidence of extraterrestrial origin or of any threat to Earth existed.

Though it is the fruit of an artist's imagination, a menacing alien model may be closer to the truth than many would wish. Physicist Stephen Hawking has warned of devastating consequences if and when aliens and humans make contact.

ous for the people of Earth. He believes that any aliens capable of reaching Earth would have to be far superior to humans in knowledge. Since they would have to cross interstellar distances to reach Earth, they would have to have abilities still impossible for humankind, such as warping space and time. Perhaps they would know how to create a portal called a wormhole through which they could travel from star to star in seconds. Hawking imagines that the extraterrestrials would be space wanderers, looking for new worlds to conquer and exploit because they had used up the resources on their own world. Their scientific capabilities and technologies would allow them to strip whole planets of natural resources and perhaps steal the power of the sun for energy, leaving Earth devastated and dead. Humans, as the vastly inferior species, would have no defense against such predatory and powerful extraterrestrials.

Hawking believes that because contact with intelligent extraterrestrials would be so risky, humans should do everything they can to hide Earth from aliens. They should not try to find intelligent extraterrestrial life and should not respond if an alien message is ever discovered. He explains, "If aliens ever visit us, I think the outcome would be much as when Christopher Columbus first landed in America, which didn't turn out very well for the Native Americans." He goes on to say, "We only have to look at ourselves to see how intelligent life might develop into something we wouldn't want to meet."[45]

Conflict Is Likely

Scientists such as Robert Ehrlich agree with Hawking that a visit by intelligent extraterrestrials would threaten Earth's inhabitants. Ehrlich, a physicist, considers examples of human behavior throughout history when he imagines how aliens might treat humans. The ability to reach Earth suggests to Ehrlich that such aliens would be far more advanced than humans. Ehrlich can imagine four ways that aliens might be able to visit Earth: They have figured out how to travel faster than the speed of light, although humans currently believe that is impossible; they send intelligent, thinking robots to do their visiting for them; they are so long-lived that the time needed for interstellar travel is unimportant to them; or they live for many generations on their ships.

Ehrlich thinks that any of these possibilities would pose a threat to humankind, if only because all represent technology and abilities that humans cannot match. In any conflict with extraterrestrials or their representatives (the robots), humans would be unable to defend themselves. He explains, "All our experiences on Earth suggest that when a more technologically advanced species or group of humans encounters another and competes for the same resources, the result is always conflict, with the more advanced group emerging victorious."[46]

Ehrlich also worries that advanced, intelligent extraterrestrials would not see humans as an intelligent, sentient species. Humans would be seen as inferior. Just as humans often classify animals as lower beings, the extraterrestrials might see humans as little more than animals and treat them without respect or compassion. He says:

> On Earth our recognition of the deep mental and emotional lives of some of our fellow passengers on the planet has come exceedingly slowly—with [seventeenth-century philosopher] Rene Descartes even holding that animals are simply robots having no thoughts or feelings. Given the probability that the gap in intelligence between alien visitors and humans would be far greater than that between humans and our close relatives on Earth, how could they not think of us as a very lowly life form, certainly not worthy of treating as equals?[47]

Communist Aliens

In the Soviet Union during the 1930s, Russian biologist and agriculture expert Trofim Lysenko publicized the theory that all advanced civilizations are peaceful, unselfish, self-sacrificing, and dedicated to the welfare of everyone. They are altruistic because any advanced society has evolved naturally to be socialist. An advanced society chooses, by definition, socialism or communism. Today, Lysenko is considered to be a fraud, but his views about the inevitable altruism of an advanced civilization linger. Physicist David Brin says that this idea of the universal altruism of advanced civilizations still affects Russian thought today. He thinks Lysenko's ideas explain why Russian scientists strongly favor trying to contact extraterrestrial civilizations. The Russian scientists think fear of hostile or menacing extraterrestrials is silly and just based on science fiction. Most of them believe that any advanced technological society must be altruistic and no threat to humankind.

Humans as Lowly Life-Forms

Perhaps aliens visiting Earth would not be hostile or aggressive toward humanity but simply not notice the life-forms so far beneath them. This could be extremely destructive for humans. At *Discover Magazine*'s science blog, physicist Sean Carroll refers to the 1996 science-fiction spoof *Mars Attacks!* in which aliens gleefully bring ruin to all that they encounter, when he comments, "If aliens were sufficiently enlightened to be utterly peace-loving and generous, it would be great to have back-and-forth contact with them. But it's also possible that they would simply wipe us out—not necessarily in a *Mars Attacks!* kind of invasion, but almost without noticing (as we have done to countless species here on Earth already)."[48] If the aliens just wanted to exploit Earth's resources, for example, they might not even be aware of the consequences to the people of Earth. They might as casually destroy humanity as a person would casually kick an anthill or step on an ant.

People might be like ants to advanced extraterrestrials, says physicist Michio Kaku. He does not expect an alien invasion anytime soon, but Kaku believes that people should start considering the possibility of advanced alien beings whose intelligence and technology far outstrips Earth's. He explains, "Maybe they're so advanced that we're not even on their radar screen. We're so arrogant to believe that they're going to want to land on the White House lawn. I mean, if you see an ant hill in the forest, you go down to the ants and say I bring you trinkets, I bring you beads. I give you nuclear energy. Take me to your ant leader. Is that what you do when you see an ant hill? I don't think so."[49]

Kaku, however, is not worried about the threat of extraterrestrials. He imagines that, as ants, humans are both uninteresting and perhaps too much trouble for aliens to bother with an Earth invasion. It does not make sense to him that aliens searching for natural resources would choose an inhabited planet. Kaku believes that they would logically choose one of the millions of Earth-like planets that are rich in resources and likely to be uninhabited. He explains, "If you're a camper, are you going to sit down where there are a lot of scorpions and tarantulas and rattlesnakes? No. You're going [to] go where it's nice and clean of pests. So why would they bother with the earth when there are lots of pristine planets with plenty of resources out there?"[50]

Not a Threat

If Kaku is right, Earth has little to fear from an extraterrestrial visit. Maybe the aliens would think of humans as pests, or maybe they would be peaceful and curious, contacting Earth to share knowledge and friendship. Either way, Kaku does not think that intelligent extraterrestrials would be a threat to humankind. On the contrary, he thinks contact with intelligent extraterrestrials would be of tremendous benefit to humankind. He believes that a profitable exchange of culture and information would result. He says, "As a scientist, I look forward to the day when we make contact with other intelligent life forms in the universe. So, rather than being frightened, I think we'd approach the idea with open arms, with open mind, realizing that this could be a turning point in the history of the human race."[51]

In the 1996 science-fiction spoof Mars Attacks! *the aliens (one of whom is pictured here) clearly enjoy destroying Earth's people and property. In real life, alien visitors to Earth might bring ruin without even realizing it, say some scientists.*

In an article titled "Why Stephen Hawking Is Wrong," Paul Davies suggests several reasons that intelligent extraterrestrials would be no threat to humankind. Assuming that intelligent life is common, Davies says, then some civilizations would have evolved millions of years ago. Long before Earth's solar system was born, many stars and planetary systems at the center of the Milky Way were already old. If intelligent life evolved on even a few of these planets, the extraterrestrials would have developed advanced civilizations and technology before humans even existed. Davies does not think it is logical to imagine that any such civilization would wait until humans evolved to decide to exploit Earth. He argues, "If resources are the motivating factor, then at least one group of aliens would surely have spotted Earth as a desirable destination millions of years ago, and come here when they could have had the planet for the asking, without pesky humans to complicate the takeover."[52]

Travel Barriers

Davies brings up another more important consideration, too: As far as scientists know, no spaceship can go faster than the speed of light. This means that travel between the stars would be effectively impossible for aliens (or humans) because it would take hundreds and thousands of years. Although people imagine warp drives and wormholes, the ideas are not supported by any scientific evidence, and Davies does not accept any theories not grounded in good science. He explains:

> The galaxy is huge by human standards. The nearest star is over four light years away—about 25 trillion miles. [A light year—the distance light travels in one year—is 5.88 trillion miles (9.46 trillion km).] Within the scientific community, even the optimists believe the nearest civilization could well be hundreds of light years away. Because nothing can travel faster than light, the Hollywood image of aliens plying the vast interstellar voids in star fleets is absurd. It's far more likely that alien civilizations would limit contact to radio communication rather than engage in the sort of close encounters favored by movie makers.[53]

A Plot to Destroy Humankind

British astronomer Fred Hoyle believed that life on Earth did not evolve spontaneously but began with microorganisms from space. Hoyle speculated that intelligent aliens from an alternate universe seeded Earth with viral gene packages. He believed they were conducting a kind of genetic experiment that resulted in the evolution of intelligent life.

In 1961, Hoyle and producer John Elliot wrote *A for Andromeda,* a television drama about hostile aliens who use a genetic experiment in order to change human evolution. In the story, aliens from the Andromeda galaxy radio a seemingly friendly message to Earth with instructions for building a supercomputer. Earthlings, anxious to acquire advanced knowledge, build the computer, which has its own agenda. It teaches Earth scientists to grow a human embryo with altered genetic information—a super-human with an alien mentality. This new human is a slave to the computer program, which is working to take over Earth, evolve alien-type humans, and destroy humankind.

The computer provided a way for the aliens to colonize space, even though they could not physically transverse interstellar distances. The Andromeda message was not information sharing but a plot to conquer. Hoyle's warning is that even an alien message could be a threat if humans are too trusting and fail to be wary.

Radio contact could not pose a direct threat to Earth. Even if aliens communicating with Earth were hostile, they would not have the ability to attack or destroy humanity since they could not travel the distance between their home planet and Earth.

Davies recognizes the possibility that Earth's scientists might be wrong about the travel barrier of the speed of light. Some scientists, for instance, believe that wormholes are hypothetically possible. However, even if space travel through a wormhole has been discovered by an advanced extraterrestrial civilization, Davies refuses to believe that a visit to Earth would be a threat. Like Kaku, he imagines that extraterrestrials would come in peace.

Davies argues that no scientific reason has been found to imagine that aliens would have evolved in the same way that humanity did. Therefore, looking at human history and evolution to predict the behavior of extraterrestrials is illogical. Humans, for example, evolved from predators, but that does not mean that all intelligent species have to be predatory. In addition, human civilization is still young. Davies wonders how much more peaceful humans might be after another million years of evolution and experience. He believes that any civilization that is millions of years old is unlikely to be hostile or destructive. He explains, "Just because we go around wiping out our competitors doesn't mean aliens would do the same. A civilization that has endured for millions of years would have overcome any aggressive tendencies, and may well have genetically engineered its species for harmonious living. Any truly bellicose [warlike] alien species would either have wiped itself out long ago, or already taken over the galaxy."[54]

The Nature of Intelligent Aliens

Physicist GianCarlo Ghirardi believes that intelligent aliens probably exist, but he does not imagine that they would be hostile. He argues that with the evolution of intelligence, compassion, ethical thought, and reason also evolve. As human civilizations have developed, so has the belief that life has value and should be treasured. Ghirardi supposes that intelligent aliens would develop similar moral traits. He says:

> Certainly these beings would realize that there is life on the earth,
> and would not be motivated to automatically enslave or destroy

other living beings, as these are rather primitive, unthinking, reactions, and not the mark of what we might expect of a higher culture and ethics. And if life is everywhere, then it might be expected that these alien wanderers would not only see it as pointless to destroy life, but might develop a respect for all the living creatures they would have met in their endless travel. Curiosity and the desire to acquire knowledge does not equate a desire to conquer and destroy.[55]

Stephen Freeland of the Institute for Astronomy at the University of Hawaii does not claim to know what intelligent aliens might be like, but he does believe that fears of intelligent extraterrestrials are unscientific. Science, he explains, must be empirical—based on the evidence of human senses and careful testing; logic and reason alone are not enough to draw conclusions about the motives of aliens. Freeland believes that scientists should not talk about aliens as threatening or nonthreatening without scientific evidence. He argues, "Thus, when Stephen Hawking (or any other scientist) find themselves speaking as a scientist on the likely nature of visiting aliens, they have a responsibility to defend the integrity of science by either demonstrating the scientific basis (empirical tests) for what is being said, or clearly explaining the other (non-scientific) credentials for their information."[56] Since humans have no information about aliens, Freeland rejects all opinions about them.

Aliens Are Not Human

Theories of aliens that are based on human experience may be flawed, some scientists say. Astronomer Harold A. Geller rejects the idea that alien minds and motives can be understood by comparing them to human minds and motives. He explains that the way extraterrestrials evolved would probably be so different from how humans evolved that no one can imagine whether they would be threatening, peaceful, or comparable to humans in any way. They would have evolved to be suited to their home planet, not Earth. Their thought processes would be alien;

their physical forms would be unlike those found on Earth; and their civilization and culture would be so different as to be unintelligible to humankind. Geller argues, "The probability that intelligent beings from another star system would share a common biology, chemistry, psychology and sociology with humans might be infinitesimally small."[57] Therefore, the aliens would not even be interested in Earth's resources. Nothing that evolved on Earth would be compatible with their physical needs or their interests and values.

Geller also cannot imagine aliens needing the energy from Earth's sun. Logically, he says, if they are so far advanced as to be able to travel among the stars, they would also be advanced enough to have protected their own world and maintained its ecology. They would be able to plan for the future and conserve their energy resources. If they did not, he

If aliens search for stars from which to mine energy, some scientists say, they are unlikely to search in our own Milky Way galaxy. The Andromeda galaxy (pictured) is thought to have more than a trillion suns and would probably have much greater appeal.

argues, where did the energy come from that they used to travel to Earth in their spaceships?

Even if aliens do need to mine the energy of stars to fuel their journeys, Geller still does not think they would choose Earth's sun. It is too small and ordinary. He explains, "Our galaxy is estimated to contain at least 500 billion stars. Andromeda [the nearest galaxy to the Milky Way] is believed to consist of over a trillion suns. If it is the energy of the sun they require, then given the rather small stature of our sun, and the greater abundance of more desirable and larger stars, it would seem the Earth and our solar system would not be of interest to alien invaders."[58]

> **DID YOU KNOW?**
>
> Some scientists suggest that aliens are not a threat because, although they know humankind exists, the aliens do not care and are completely uninterested in Earth life or its resources.

No One Knows for Certain

Even with no scientific evidence about the nature of alien intelligence, scientists continue to speculate and argue about whether humanity should welcome or fear the idea of extraterrestrial contact. No matter how logical the arguments, no one can know for sure who is right. Physicist Peter Sturrock can see both sides of the argument over whether intelligent aliens might be a threat to Earth. He says:

Any species that has a secure and happy home may well have a benevolent attitude towards our adolescent civilization on Earth, but any species that is on a dying planet, and is desperately trying to find somewhere else to live, may not have our best interests at heart. To look on the bright side—advanced civilizations may have a code of ethics that would give us some protection. But—to look on the dark side—they may not."[59]

What should humanity do? Since many scientists who study the universe believe that intelligent aliens are likely to exist, most of them think that some kind of contact with aliens is inevitable in the future. Even if it does not happen in the lifetimes of most people now, it will happen for future generations. If that is so, then humanity should begin to prepare for the day that extraterrestrials and humans meet. Earthlings should be gathering as much information as possible—listening for radio signals in the galaxy, exploring with probes, using space telescopes to identify habitable planets and their characteristics—so that humanity can plan its response when contact is made. People will have to determine whether to answer messages from intelligent aliens or hide; whether to prepare defenses against them or greet them in friendship. These are undecided issues today, but of one thing scientists are sure: The more knowledge we have, the better.

CHAPTER FOUR

Making Contact

Unless a superpowerful alien invasion force suddenly appears in the skies above Earth, humankind has some choices about how and if it will make contact with any extraterrestrial intelligence. What to do should the chance of contact ever come is a serious topic of discussion and debate among scientists, philosophers, and other thoughtful people around the world.

Detecting a Signal

Imagine, says Paul Davies, that on a perfectly ordinary day a bored young astronomer at the SETI Institute is sitting out his shift, monitoring the radio telescope as it methodically scans the skies. The astronomer is lazing in front of his detection instruments, just as he has so many days before. Suddenly a computer-generated alarm sounds. "At first," says Davies, "the astronomer assumes that it's just another one of those false alarms." So he follows SETI protocol and moves the telescope away from the received signal, sees the signal die out, and then moves the telescope back "on target and the signal is still there."[60] It looks like a purposeful signal from an alien intelligence. However, the astronomer has to confirm that the signal is not just radio noise from space or an Earth satellite. Will a faraway telescope pick up the same signal? He sends the coordinates to another SETI observatory so they will know where to aim their telescope.

Davies continues:

> Five thousand miles away, another astronomer is called out of bed to investigate. Drowsily she wanders to the control room and pours herself a coffee. Then . . . she enters the given coordinates. Within a minute the second radio telescope has locked onto the target and immediately picks up the same signal, loud and clear. Her pulse begins to race. Is it conceivable that this time the alert is for real? . . . She knows that many more checks will be needed before leaping to [conclusions], but the two astronomers, now in excited telephone conversation between different continents, systematically eliminate one mundane possibility after another until, with 90 per cent certainty, they infer that the signal is indeed artificial, non-human, and originating far, far out in space. . . . What next? Who to tell? What can be gleaned from the data already gathered? *Will the world ever be the same again?*[61]

SETI Post-Detection Protocol

Because of those questions, the SETI Institute established the SETI Post-Detection Taskgroup in 2001. Davies is its current chairperson. The taskgroup does not have the force of law, is not a part of any government, and cannot give orders about what scientists should do if they discover a message or signal from extraterrestrial life. The group's job is to prepare for that day and provide advice to scientists about what to do after the message is detected. Davies calls the job a huge and important responsibility.

The taskgroup advises that first the discoverers of the signal should carefully check and confirm that the signal is genuinely an alien, artificial signal. This is a step that could take many days, during which the news

The 140-foot Green Bank radio telescope in West Virginia was part of a network of telescopes used by SETI Institute researchers. Radio telescopes such as this one scan the skies in search of signals from extraterrestrial beings.

of the supposed message should not be leaked to anyone. Then, when the astronomers are sure the alien signal is real, they should report the discovery to other astronomers through their worldwide association, the International Astronomical Union (IAU). The IAU would then inform the United Nations. The astronomer who received the signal would next inform his or her government—the country in which the radio telescope is located. Other governments would be informed by the IAU. Only then would the astronomers who discovered the message hold a press conference and inform the world that humankind is not alone in the galaxy. The taskgroup cannot be sure that individual astronomers will follow their planned steps. "However," says Davies, "the most likely scenario is that a detection event comes from within the SETI community, and in that case the Taskgroup's protocol is likely to be adhered to, and its advice heeded. Anyway, that's the theory."[62]

Who Speaks for Earth?

The taskgroup and the SETI Institute believe that the public should be made aware of such momentous events when they occur. Davies says that no one in SETI or among the members of the Post-Detection Taskgroup believe in secrecy. Public openness, however, creates a large problem because someone has to decide what to do. This question is so serious for humankind that Davies argues that one fact should be kept secret—at least for a while: The actual coordinates in space from which the message came. No responsible scientist wants random people to start beaming signals and messages back to aliens. The major issue, Davies explains, is that no one person has the right to make decisions about contacting alien intelligence. Humanity, as a whole, must decide: "Should we respond? If so, what should we say? Above all, who speaks for Earth?"[63] Some people argue that whether and how to

DID YOU KNOW?

The character played by Jodie Foster in the 1997 movie *Contact* is based on real-life SETI Institute director Jill Tarter.

Foolish Earthlings

At one time the SETI project was part of NASA, supported with government funds. Then, in 1979 Wisconsin senator William Proxmire gave SETI a "Golden Fleece Award." It was his way of publicizing government programs that he thought were wasteful and fleeced American taxpayers. By 1981 Proxmire had persuaded the Senate to discontinue SETI funding, arguing the search was foolish and that "there is not a scintilla of evidence that intelligent life exists beyond our solar system." NASA scientist Charles Redmond retorted, "As late as 1491 there was not a scintilla of evidence that America existed." Proxmire did not listen.

Carl Sagan, then one of the most well known and respected scientists in America, visited Proxmire and begged him to reconsider his stance. Sagan was able to convince Proxmire that the program was real science. Funding was restored and continued until 1992, when the Senate again halted all SETI funding due to budget concerns. Today SETI is privately funded, and neither the federal government nor NASA is involved in the decision making or the search.

Quoted in John Kraus, "People and Places: Proxmire vs. SETI," *Cosmic Search*, issue 13, vol. 4, no. 1, 1982. www.bigear.org.

respond should be an international decision. Others argue that scientists, perhaps NASA scientists, are in the best position to compose an answer to a message. So far, however, who speaks for Earth has not been decided.

Jill Tarter, the director of the SETI Institute's Mountain View, California, research center, explains that SETI scientists have not really made plans beyond how to confirm and announce that an alien radio signal has been received. "Then," she says, "I don't know what happens."[64] The scientists searching for radio signals have talked about what to do; they generally agree that the finding should be reported publicly; and they do believe that they should not transmit an answer. However, they have no idea who, if anyone, should speak for Earth or who should be able to decide whether to respond to the signal or who should decide what the reply would be.

One SETI project, called Earth Speaks, is an effort to include the world's ordinary people in the decision-making process and in choosing the kind of message that humanity wants to send back to an alien civilization. Earth Speaks was designed and organized by SETI Institute scientist Douglas Vakoch. The SETI Institute has held meetings with various scholars and scientists for years about how Earth should respond if an extraterrestrial signal is detected. Vakoch and others, however, decided to set up a study to identify the kinds of messages suggested by people from all walks of life. The study is based on the idea that a message from Earth to aliens should be from all humankind, not just a few leaders or scientists. At the Earth Speaks website, Vakoch and his team invite people from all over the world to submit ideas for messages that they would like to send to extraterrestrials. The site allows people to vote on the appropriateness of the suggestions it receives. The scientists of Earth Speaks will try to identify the major themes of the messages and combine these themes into a statement about what humanity wants to say. The goal of Earth Speaks is to provide any extraterrestrials with a representative picture of humanity. The project also asks people to comment on whether Earth should reply at all to an alien message. Many contributors to Earth Speaks suggest friendly replies, but others are not so sure.

DID YOU KNOW?

At every telescope site where they work, SETI Institute scientists keep a bottle of champagne on ice, ready to celebrate the detection of a real alien signal.

To Answer or Not?

Whether to respond to an alien message or to maintain silence is controversial among scientists, too. Stephen Hawking's view is clear: Don't talk to aliens. Astronomer Zdenek Kopal voiced the same warning years before Hawking did. He said, "Should we ever hear the space-phone ringing, for God's sake let us not answer, but rather make ourselves as inconspicuous as possible to avoid attracting attention!"[65] Tarter agrees that the decision to reply to any message should be made with extreme caution. Earth and its sun are very young in comparison to the age of the galaxy. This means, she says, that human civilization is likely to be the youngest civilization in the galaxy and, therefore, the most vulnerable. The safest thing to do is to listen, try to decode the message, learn everything possible about extraterrestrial intelligence, and keep quiet.

Some scientists, however, do not want to play it safe. Physicist Ethan Siegel, for instance, says he is eager to communicate with any extraterrestrials and does not agree with those who fear contact. He argues, "But what irks me most of all is the cowardice behind a viewpoint that we shouldn't rush to meet a peer in this Universe. It would be like forgetting the best part of being human: our bravery, our sense of adventure, our will to explore, our thirst for learning and discovery, our curiosity, and our desire to experience all that existence has to offer."[66] Other scientists predict that alien contact and information exchange would be of great benefit, advancing Earth's science and technology and increasing humanity's understanding of the universe.

Communication Across Deep Space

Poul Anderson was a science-fiction writer and adviser to the SETI League—a group of amateur astronomers from around the world who are searching the skies for evidence of intelligent life. Before he died in 2001, Anderson was a strong supporter of the search for extraterrestrial intelligence and of progressing—should the chance ever come—from SETI (the search for extraterrestrial intelligence) to CETI (communication with extraterrestrial intelligence). He said, "To make contact will simply be a wonderful beginning." However, he pointed out that detection of a signal or message does not mean immediate interaction and replies. Anderson argued that understanding and decoding any alien message will be so difficult that no one need fear the threat of alien contact

Twitters to Extraterrestrials

Ian O'Neill, an astronomer and science producer for Discovery News, believes that active SETI is important and necessary to advance human knowledge of the galaxy. He supports sending radio messages into space, but he says that if Earth is ever to get a reply, humans must make the messages as interesting and attractive as possible. He thinks boring messages, such as mathematical formulas, might be ignored by intelligent extraterrestrials. Messages that simply announce human presence might be boring, too.

Messages should impart interesting facts about humankind. O'Neill recommends that scientists take a lesson from Twitter and transmit short messages that are full of fascinating information. He says brief but information-rich messages (140 characters long, like Twitter messages) are the best way to make new friends. Perhaps the messages would describe the best things about Earth's people—what their art is like or how their science explains space-time or what their philosophers think about life. The messages would be positive because positive, interesting tweets attract others and collect friends. With twitter messages in the "twitter-verse," says O'Neill, Earth would be "seen as an island of interesting, intelligent beings." Aliens would want to reply.

Ian O'Neill, "Could Active SETI Learn from . . . Twitter?" Astroengine.com, April 21, 2009. www.astroengine.com.

for a long time, if ever. He imagined, "If ever SETI succeeds, CETI will then stretch over a period of years, decades, or quite possibly centuries. An organization dedicated to it may become something like a church, outliving nations as it carries on its magnificent mission."[67]

Vakoch has another reason not to fear communicating with aliens. He thinks they are just too far away to be a threat. Vakoch asks, "Even if they tend to be hateful, awful folks, can they do us any harm at interstellar distances?"[68] If an alien message had to travel light years, it could be hundreds or thousands of years before it reached Earth, and any reply would take hundreds or thousands of years to get back to the extraterrestrials. Then, even if the aliens were hostile and wanted to travel to Earth, Vakoch argues, it would be illogical to imagine they would do so just to wage war or steal Earth's resources. The cost of such an expedition—in time and energy—would be prohibitive.

Seth Shostak thinks the whole argument about hiding from alien contact is useless anyway. It is too late to hide. For decades, he explains, military radar signals and radio and television shows have been beaming from Earth into space. These transmissions are called "leakage" and are a result of a modern technology that produces radio waves. These signals fade after they have traveled a few light years into space and could not be picked up by technology equivalent to current radio telescopes on Earth. However, earthlings are capable of building a telescope array that could pick up the radio signals from a great interstellar distance, and so could any advanced alien civilization. If such exists, it already knows that Earth is home to an intelligent civilization. Shostak says, "This horse has left the barn. Any society that could possibly be a threat to us can easily know at least that we're here. There's no point in losing sleep over this."[69]

> ### DID YOU KNOW?
>
> In September 2010 news outlets reported that the United Nations had appointed Malaysian astrophysicist Mazlan Othman to be Earth's first ambassador to aliens. Othman and the UN, however, deny the reports.

Calling All Extraterrestrials

Russian radar astronomer Alexander Zaitsev argues that if everyone fears that extraterrestrials could be a threat, "Our civilization would be doomed to eternal silence."[70] Humans would never respond to a message or contact any alien civilization because they could never be certain whether the message came from a hostile civilization or a peaceful one. Zaitsev believes that humanity should respond if a message ever comes, but he goes even further. He wants people to expand the search for alien life by sending messages into space and thereby announcing the presence of human civilization and inviting contact. This idea is called "active SETI" or METI (messaging to extraterrestrial intelligence). Some SETI scientists, perhaps frustrated by the failure to find any radio signals from alien civilizations, have also suggested that powerful radio signals should be beamed from Earth into space in an effort to make contact.

Active SETI has already been done on a small scale. During the 1970s the *Pioneer* and *Voyager* probes were launched with information about Earth and its inhabitants. The two *Pioneer* probes carried small metal plaques identifying the time and place of origin. The two *Voyager* probes carried a 12-inch (30cm) gold-plated phonograph record intended to communicate a story of Earth to extraterrestrials. It included natural sounds such as those made by surf, thunder, and birds; music from different cultures and eras; and spoken greetings in 55 languages. These probes are not aimed at a particular star system but have begun to drift outside the solar system into deep space. If any extraterrestrial intelligence finds the probes, they will discover a message from Earth. In 1974 astronomers used the Arecibo radio telescope in Puerto Rico to send a series of radio pulses toward a group of stars called the M13 cluster, 25,000 light years from Earth, in a kind of mathematical message. (The soonest that Earth could receive a reply would be in 50,000 years.) More recently, beginning in 1999, Zaitsev has used the Evpatoria telescope in Ukraine to send radio signals to nearby stars in the hope that one will be received by an alien civilization. And in 2001 Zaitsev transmitted the "Teen-Age Message to the Stars." A group of Russian teenagers helped him compose a message, complete with music, to beam to six nearby stars. (A reply from these signals could reach Earth in a couple hundred years.)

> ## DID YOU KNOW?
>
> In 2008 a radio antenna in Madrid, Spain, was used to transmit the Beatles' song "Across the Universe" toward the North Star, Polaris, 431 light years distant from Earth.

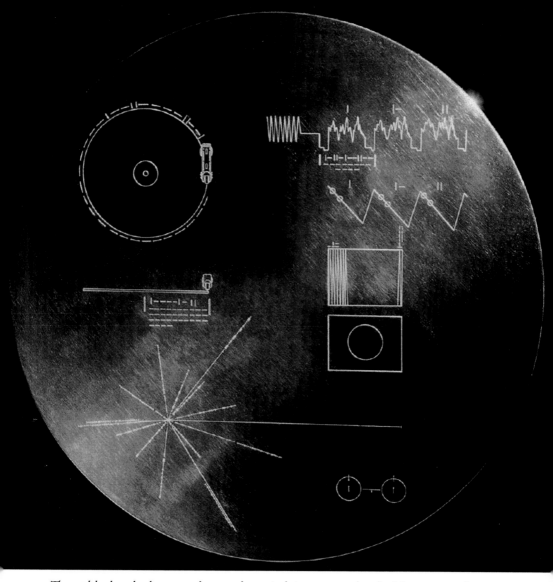

The gold-plated phonograph record carried into space by the Voyager *probes contains various sights and sounds of Earth. Its cover (pictured) also provides information. In the upper left-hand corner is a drawing of a phonograph record, with the stylus in the correct position to play the record from the beginning. Among other images is a drawing in the lower left-hand corner showing the location of the solar system with respect to 14 pulsars.*

Zaitsev and his colleagues Charles Chafer and Richard Braastad believe that people have nothing to fear from sending messages from Earth out into the universe. They envision the benefits that contact could bring to humanity. For instance, they argue that the knowledge and wisdom from an advanced extraterrestrial civilization might help humankind survive. Perhaps humans would learn to live in peace or to avoid nuclear war or how to save the environment from pollution or global warming. To those scientists who want to listen but not transmit, they say, "Suppose each extraterrestrial civilization in the Milky Way has been frightened by its own SETI leaders into believing that sending messages to other stars is just too risky. Then it is possible we live in a galaxy where everyone is listening and no one is speaking. In order to learn of each others' existence—and science—someone has to make the first move."[71]

Safety First

Most SETI scientists, however, are disturbed by active SETI. They believe that a small group of scientists has no right to make decisions that could affect everyone on Earth. Physicist and science-fiction writer David Brin, for example, considers METI efforts to be "A path that might have serious consequences to humanity."[72] He says that justifications in favor of METI are nothing more than arrogance and unsupported theories from a small group of people who think they know best.

Brin says that astronomers who want to beam strong signals in order to make Earth's civilization highly visible are taking a terrible risk, based on nothing but the belief that extraterrestrial civilizations are highly evolved, peaceful, and friendly. Brin calls METI "shouting at the cosmos." He says, "If aliens are so advanced and altruistic . . . and yet are choosing to remain silent . . . should we not consider following their example and doing likewise? At least for a little while? Is it possible that they are silent because they know something we don't know?"[73]

Carl Sagan and one of SETI's first researchers, Philip Morrison, also argued against METI. Both scientists recommended that earthlings search and listen but not send signals into space. Both men believed that human civilization is too young and ignorant of the universe to aggressively try to contact extraterrestrial civilizations. Brin states: "The newest children in a strange and uncertain cosmos should listen quietly for a long time, patiently learning about the universe and comparing notes, before shouting into an unknown jungle that we do not understand."[74] He argues that the METI scientists are gambling with the future of humankind to prove that their beliefs are correct.

Brin also does not agree with the argument that Earth's radio transmissions have already revealed human presence. He explains that the galaxy is so large that aliens may simply not yet have looked in the right place to discover Earth. It is not too late, Brin maintains, to keep silent and be cautious. He says,

> A parallel might be the way we sometimes screen our [phone] calls, listening to messages instead of answering right away. What we almost never do (past the age of twelve), is just punch random numbers into the phone, jabbering at anyone who happens to be out there, telling them our names and where we live. We certainly don't go roaming about, shouting, in the darkest part of an unknown town.[75]

At the very least, Brin argues, the decision to engage in active SETI should be made by the whole scientific community and perhaps all Earth's people rather than by a few scientists. He says, "Certainly the general public . . . deserve to hear all sides. Especially since it is their posterity that (under some worried views of the universe) may ultimately be on the line."[76]

The Real Threat?

METI represents a strong determination to make contact with extraterrestrial intelligence, but perhaps, it, too, will fail. Maybe, if intelligent aliens exist, they refuse to make contact with Earth. Psychiatrist Rhawn

Joseph has an idea about why no alien intelligence has made contact. "Perhaps," he speculates, "like good anthropologists they merely observe and gather information, and for the most part leave Earthlings to behave largely unmolested. Speculating wildly, maybe it is even against some type of Cosmic law. Or there is little or no motivation to visit a world that is just like a trillion other planets swarming with violent, sex-obsessed, power-hungry human-like creatures."[77]

Aliens could even be afraid of humanity. Humans have been aggressive toward each other throughout history. Given the chance, perhaps humanity would attack, exploit, or enslave any aliens that tried to make contact. Davies is not worried about METI, but he does think that humans could be a threat to aliens. If aliens are aware of humans but do not want to make contact, Davies thinks humankind ought to respect that decision. Perhaps the aliens are right that human civilization is not advanced enough to be accepted as part of any interstellar community. Davies speculates that the only true danger from intelligent aliens would be their seeing Earth as a threat to the galaxy. Then, humanity could be in trouble.

Davies believes that predatory aliens are unlikely, but he does imagine one perilous scenario for humankind. He wonders if humanity's aggressive tendencies and history of war and violence might be incompatible with an interstellar association of peaceful aliens. If intelligent extraterrestrial communities exist, Davies hypothesizes that they have outgrown conflict and war or perhaps never evolved to be aggressive. In either case, the aliens might see humans as too primitive to be welcomed into their community. They might worry that exploitive, destructive humans are a threat to the peace of the galaxy. If humans seem to be on the threshold of space travel, Davies wonders if the alien community would attack and destroy humankind in self-defense. Perhaps, he says, humankind should stay on Earth until its civilization has become more peaceful and abandoned its violent ways. Otherwise, Earth may be viewed as a menace to other galactic inhabitants. He says, "Ironically, the greatest danger from an alien encounter may be ourselves."[78]

SOURCE NOTES

Introduction: Unknown Dangers

1. James Garvin, *Alien Planet*, directed by Pierre de Lespinois, produced by John Copeland, 2005; Evergreen Films LLC for Discovery Communications, Discovery Channel/Gaiam.
2. Michio Kaku, *Alien Planet*.
3. J. Craig Venter, *Alien Planet*.

Chapter One: Is Any Kind of Life Out There?

4. Quoted in Paul Davies, *The Eerie Silence: Renewing Our Search for Alien Intelligence*. New York: Houghton Mifflin Harcourt, 2010, p. 25.
5. Quoted in Paul Davies, *The Eerie Silence*, p. 31.
6. Stephen Hawking, *Alien Planet*.
7. NASA Astrobiology, "About Astrobiology," January 21, 2008. http://astrobiology.nasa.gov.
8. NASA, "The Mars Exploration Program: Program Overview." www.nasa.gov.
9. Quoted in Phoenix Mars Mission, "Phoenix Mars Lander Is Silent, New Image Shows Damage," May 24, 2010. http://phoenix.lpl.arizona.edu.
10. Quoted in *European Union Times*, "Meteorites from Mars Contain Ancient Fossils," *EU Times* Online, May 9, 2010. www.eutimes.net.
11. Quoted in Victoria Jaggard, "Could Jupiter Moon Harbor Fish-Size Life?" *National Geographic News*, November 16, 2009.
12. Quoted in Emma Harding, "Could Life Exist on Jupiter Moon?" BBC Radio 4, February 4, 2010. http://news.bbc.co.uk.
13. NASA Science, "The Goldilocks Zone," Science News, October 2, 2003. http://science.nasa.gov.

14. Seth Shostak, "Seth Shostak of the SETI Institute Interviewed by Sander Olson," August 18, 2010, Next Big Future.com. http://next bigfuture.com.

15. Shostak, "Seth Shostak of the SETI Institute Interviewed by Sander Olson."

16. SETI Institute, "Our Mission." www.seti.org.

17. Seth Shostak, "When Will We Find the Extraterrestrials?" *Engineering and Science,* Spring 2009, p.18. http://archive.seti.org.

18. Shostak, "When Will We Find the Extraterrestrials?" p. 18.

19. Carl Sagan, "The Quest for Extraterrestrial Intelligence," *Smithsonian Magazine*, May 1978, repr., Cosmic Quest. www.kejvmen.sk.

20. Quoted in Mindgangsta, "'The Great Silence'—Stephen Hawking & Others Look at Why Life Has Yet to Be Discovered Beyond Earth," February 28, 2010. http://mindgangsta.wordpress.com.

21. Quoted in James Schombert, "Lecture 26: Fermi's Paradox," Cosmology, University of Oregon, December 1, 2008. http://abyss.u oregon.edu.

22. Kaku, *Alien Planet*.

23. Paul Davies, *The Eerie Silence*, pp. 33, 65.

Chapter Two: The Threat from Microscopic Life

24. Quoted in Canadian Space Agency, "Dr. Carpentier: Apollo Flight Surgeon," Space Medicine: Canada's Aerospace Medicine Pioneers, August 18, 2006. www.asc-csa.gc.ca.

25. Quoted in NASA Science, "Earth Microbes on the Moon," Science News, September 1, 1998. http://science.nasa.gov.

26. Rhawn Joseph and Chandra Wickramasinghe, "Comets and Contagion: Evolution and Diseases from Space," *Journal of Cosmology*, vol. 7, May 2010, pp. 1750–70. http://journalofcosmology.com.

27. Joseph and Wickramasinghe, "Comets and Contagion."

28. Joseph and Wickramasinghe, "Comets and Contagion."

29. Quoted in Nigel Hawkes, "The Threat from Life on Mars," *Sunday Times* (London), December 3, 2004. www.timesonline.co.uk.

30. Abigail A. Salyers, "Looking for Life on Mars and Beyond," American Institute of Biological Sciences, August 2004. www.actionbioscience.org.

31. Task Group on Issues in Sample Return, National Research Council, *Mars Sample Return: Issues and Recommendations*. Washington, DC: National Academies Press, 1997.

32. John Rummel, "John Rummel: Protecting the Planets from Earth Invaders," interview by Matt Kaplan, Planetary Radio, July 10, 2006. www.planetary.org.

33. Quoted in Anuradha K. Herath, "How to Protect Other Planets from Earth Microbes," *Astrobiology Magazine*, October 15, 2009. www.space.com.

34. Quoted in Adam Mann, "The SciCom Interview: John Rummel," Science Communication Program, University of California at Santa Cruz, 2010. http://scicom.ucsc.edu/Q&A/2010/rummel.php.

35. NASA Planetary Protection. http://planetaryprotection.nasa.gov.

36. Catharine A. Conley, "Planetary Protection for Mars Sample Return 4/21/08," NASA presentation. www.lpi.usra.edu.

37. Quoted in Herath, "How to Protect Other Planets from Earth Microbes."

38. Laura Woodmansee, "Planetary Protection: Saying Hello to Alien Life, Safely," SpaceDaily, September 10, 2001. www.spacedaily.com.

39. Quoted in Woodmansee, "Planetary Protection."

40. Margaret S. Race and Richard O. Randolph, "The Need for Operating Guidelines and a Decision Making Framework Applicable to the Discovery of Non-Intelligent Extraterrestrial Life," *Advances in Space Research*, vol. 30, no. 6, pp. 1583–91, 2002. www.aaas.org.

41. B.G. Sidharth, "Hawking's Alien Invaders Might Be Microorganisms," Commentaries: Stephen Hawking's Aliens, *Journal of Cosmology*, vol. 7, May, 2010, pp. 1777–94. http://journalofcosmology.com.

Chapter Three: The Threat from Intelligent Extraterrestrials

42. Chandra Wickramasinghe, "Are Intelligent Aliens a Threat to Humanity? Diseases (Viruses, Bacteria) from Space," *Journal of*

Cosmology, vol. 7, May 2010, pp. 1777–94. http://journalofcosmology.com.

43. Wickramasinghe, "Are Intelligent Aliens a Threat to Humanity?" pp. 1777–94.

44. Quoted in BBC News, "Stephen Hawking Warns over Making Contact with Aliens," April 25, 2010. http://news.bbc.co.uk.

45. Quoted in Fay Schlesinger, "Stephen Hawking: Earth Could Be at Risk of an Invasion by Aliens Living in 'Massive Ships,'" *Daily Mail* (London), April 26, 2010. www.dailymail.co.uk.

46. Robert Ehrlich, "3. Alien Conquistadors? Hawking Is Right," Commentaries: Stephen Hawking's Aliens, *Journal of Cosmology*, vol. 7, May 2010, pp. 1777–94. http://journalofcosmology.com.

47. Ehrlich, "3. Alien Conquistadors? Hawking Is Right."

48. Sean Carroll, "Hawking: Beware the Alien Menace!" Blogs/Cosmic Variance, *Discover*, April 25, 2010. http://blogs.discovermagazine.com.

49. Michio Kaku, interview by Larry King, "Stephen Hawking's Warning on Space Aliens," transcript, *Larry King Live*, CNN, May 9, 2010. http://transcripts.cnn.com.

50. Kaku, "Stephen Hawking's Warning on Space Aliens."

51. Kaku, *Alien Planet*.

52. Paul Davies, "Alien Invasion: Why Stephen Hawking Is Wrong," Speakeasy, *Wall Street Journal*, April 27, 2010. http://blogs.wsj.com.

53. Davies, "Alien Invasion: Why Stephen Hawking Is Wrong."

54. Davies, "Alien Invasion: Why Stephen Hawking Is Wrong."

55. GianCarlo Ghirardi, "9. Why Should Hawking's Aliens Wish to Destroy?" Commentaries: Stephen Hawking's Aliens, *Journal of Cosmology*, vol. 7, May 2010, pp. 1777–94. http://journalofcosmology.com.

56. Stephen Freeland, "10. The Dangers of Anti-Science: Stephen Hawking's Fear of Dangerous Aliens," Commentaries: Stephen Hawking's Aliens, *Journal of Cosmology*, vol. 7, May 2010, pp. 1777–94. http://journalofcosmology.com.

57. Harold A. Geller, "12. Stephen Hawking Is Wrong. Earth Would Not Be a Target for Alien Conquest," Commentaries: Stephen Hawking's

Aliens, *Journal of Cosmology*, vol. 7, May 2010, pp. 1777–94. http://journalofcosmology.com.

58. Geller, "12. Stephen Hawking Is Wrong. Earth Would Not be a Target for Alien Conquest."

59. Peter Sturrock, "13. Uninvited Guests," Commentaries: Stephen Hawking's Aliens, *Journal of Cosmology*, vol. 7, May 2010, pp. 1777–94. http://journalofcosmology.com.

Chapter Four: Making Contact

60. Davies, *The Eerie Silence*, p. 3.

61. Davies, *The Eerie Silence*, pp. 3–4.

62. Davies, *The Eerie Silence*, p. 170.

63. Davies, *The Eerie Silence*, p. 196.

64. Jill Tarter, "Big Think Interview with Jill Tarter, Big Think.com, June 25, 2010. http://bigthink.com.

65. Quoted in Gwynne Dyer, "Do We Really Want to Find Alien Life Forms?" *Otago Daily Times* (New Zealand), May 5, 2010. www.odt.co.nz.

66. Quoted in Patrick J. Kiger, "Months Later, Scientists Still Debating Hawking's Warning Not to Contact Alien Civilizations," *Story of the Week*, Science Channel, 2010. http://science.discovery.com.

67. Poul Anderson, "From SETI to CETI," Guest Editorial, SETI League, from *SearchLites Newsletter*, Autumn 2000. www.setileague.org.

68. Quoted in Clara Moskowitz, "Do We Dare Let Aliens Know We're Here?" MSNBC.com, August 17, 2010. www.msnbc.msn.com.

69. Quoted in Moskowitz, "Do We Dare Let Aliens Know We're Here?"

70. Alexander Zaitsev, "The SETI Paradox," *Bulletin of the Special Astrophysical Observatory*, vol. 60, 2006, p. 4. http://arxiv.org.

71. Alexander Zaitsev, Charles M. Chafer, and Richard Braastad, "Making a Case for METI," SETI League Guest Editorial, SETI League, March 5, 2005. www.setileague.org.

72. David Brin, "Shouting at the Cosmos . . . or How SETI Has Taken a Worrisome Turn into Dangerous Territory," David Brin.com, 2006. www.davidbrin.com.

73. Brin, "Shouting at the Cosmos."

74. Brin, "Shouting at the Cosmos."

75. David Brin, "A Contrarian Perspective on Altruism: The Dangers of First Contact," SETI League, September 2002. www.setileague.org.

76. Brin, "Shouting at the Cosmos."

77. Rhawn Joseph, "14. Evolution and Alien Visitors from the Stars," Commentaries: Stephen Hawking's Aliens, *Journal of Cosmology*, vol. 7, May 2010, pp. 1777–94.

78. Davies, "Alien Invasion: Why Stephen Hawking Is Wrong."

FOR FURTHER EXPLORATION

Books

Ray Jayawardhana, *Strange New Worlds: The Search for Alien Planets and Life Beyond Our Solar System*. Princeton, NJ: Princeton University Press, 2011.

T.S. Lee, *The Stephen Hawking Story: The First Stephen Hawking Comic Biography*. Englewood Cliffs, NJ: Joyful Stories/Dasan, 2010.

Seth Shostak, *Confessions of an Alien Hunter: A Scientist's Search for Extraterrestrial Intelligence*. Des Moines, IA: National Geographic, 2009.

Alvin Silverstein, Virginia B. Silverstein, and Laura Silverstein Nunn, *The Universe*. Minneapolis: Twenty-First Century, 2009.

Pamela S. Turner, *Life on Earth—and Beyond: An Astrobiologist's Quest*. Watertown, MA: Charlesbridge, 2008.

Websites

Figure the Odds of Finding ET (www.msnbc.msn.com). Visitors to this MSNBC calculator page can use the Drake Equation to make their own estimates of the number of extraterrestrial civilizations that might be broadcasting in the Milky Way.

NASA Kepler Mission (www.nasa.gov). At NASA's official Kepler mission website, visitors can learn about the search for habitable planets and the latest discoveries.

Planet Quest: NASA Jet Propulsion Laboratory (JPL) (http://planet quest.jpl.nasa.gov). At this very large website, NASA and JPL describe the exoplanet search. Click the New Worlds Atlas link for a list of every planet found so far and a description of its sun and what the planet might be like.

Professor Stephen W. Hawking (www.hawking.org.uk). This is Stephen Hawking's official website. Learn about his life, his disability, and his interests and activities.

SETI Institute (www.seti.org). This is the SETI Institute's website. Click the links from the Home page to learn about the SETI mission, astrobiology, and the latest SETI news.

The Subsurface Life in Mineral Environments (SLIME) Team (http://caveslime.org). Penelope Boston, Diana Northrup, and their team maintain this website about caves, the extremophiles in caves, and their cave explorations and discoveries.

INDEX

PICTURE CREDITS

ABOUT THE AUTHOR

Toney Allman has degrees from Ohio State University and the University of Hawaii. She currently lives in Virginia where she enjoys a rural lifestyle and researches and writes books for students on a variety of scientific and medical topics.